MERRY ENGLAND plc

By the same author

My God
But Its My Turn To Leave You
How About A Little Quarrel Before Bed?
Its Only You That's Incompatible
Calman At The Movies

Merrie England plc

calman

Mandarin

A Mandarin Paperback

MERRIE ENGLAND PLC

First published in Great Britain 1990
by Mandarin Paperbacks
Michelin House, 81 Fulham Road, London SW3 6RB

Mandarin is an imprint of the Octopus Publishing Group

Copyright © Mel Calman 1990

A CIP catalogue record for this title
is available from the British Library
ISBN 0 7493 0467 7

Printed and bound in Great Britain
by St Edmundsbury Press Limited, Bury St Edmunds, Suffolk

Introduction

We live in exciting times. Berlin knocked its wall down, Eastern Europe discovered Democracy and Merrie England plc. registered for Poll Tax. Some nights I can hardly restrain myself, so great is my need to throw my pencil at the blank sheet of paper. I drive to *The Times* with my head full of pungent words and images about the crazy world we live in.

Then I slowly wend my way through the car park, tripping over some new built debris, saunter by the Back Bench, nodding graciously to the sub editors and get to my desk. The Art Director says hello, Peter Brookes always says, 'And what time do you call this?' and I begin the creative process.

This consists of putting off for as long as possible actually putting any thoughts on paper. I read various papers. I talk to the Deputy Editor about possible topics. I open any letters from readers – and remind myself to answer both of them one day, when I'm not so harrassed. At last I approach the blank sheet of paper. I do my cartoon. I show it to my superiors – who either like it or seem to have no sense of humour at all.

I go home – avoiding the desire to go back and do something different. And then the next morning I look at the printed cartoon and wish they hadn't placed it so close to the huge photograph of Mrs Thatcher.

NEW!!
THE 90's!!
WITH ADDED HOPE & OPTIMISM!
Democracy FOR EVERYONE!!
Sounds like they're selling SHARES in it...

We must like GORBY, mustn't we?
MAGGIE TO VISIT RUSSIA
Does the other 'we' know about this?
QUEEN TO VISIT RUSSIA?

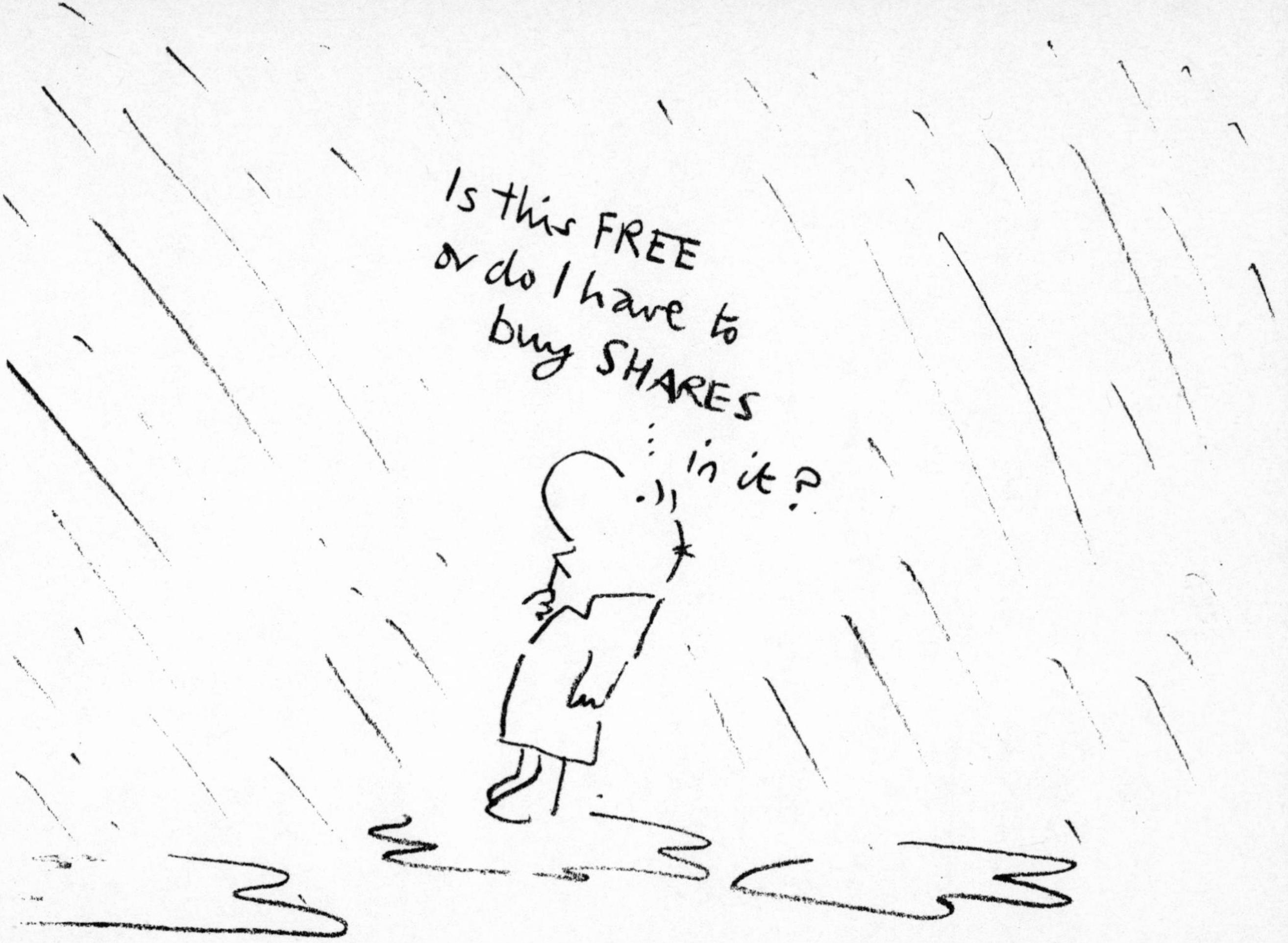
Is this FREE
or do I have to
buy SHARES
... in it?

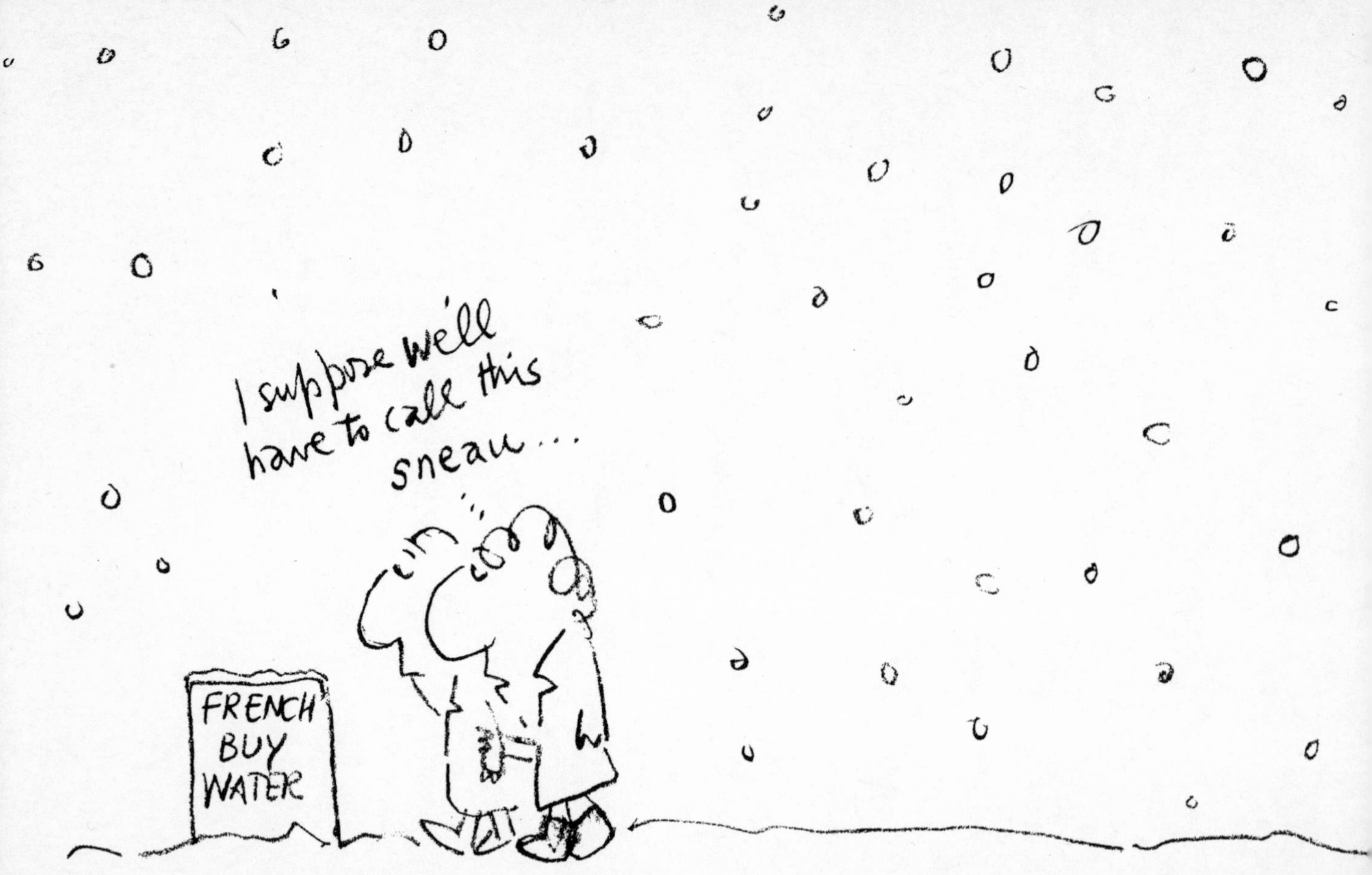
I suppose we'll have to call this sneau...
FRENCH BUY WATER

I told MUM
WATER was
bad for my
HEALTH

Run for
your lives—
we're being
liberated.

Are you saying these STONES were knocked down BEFORE you came here?

When you turn off the heating - is that GREENNESS or MEANNESS?

Lge. board –
ideal for
Conversion to
Des. Res. . . .
. . . . . .

Now RELAX -
I'm not going VANDALIZE you -
all I want is to
TALK..
They all say that!
Nothing to be
NERVOUS about -
I'll just PICK
you up -
GIVE you
some money..
It's not
UNPLEASANT..
it won't
HURT...

HELLO- hello!!
HELLO!
It's DEAD-
say something-
even if its-
'only
999
calls'...
DAMN!
I only wanted to
TALK - just felt
a BIT lonely-
it's
not
a
CRIME
is it?
CHEEK! They're
all the SAME-
let one do it
and they'll
all be
WANTING
to USE
me...

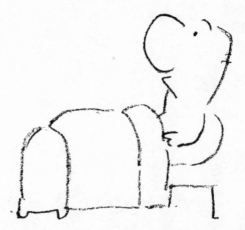

Can't you get someone to LIBEL you?
BILL
BANK
INTEREST RATES UP!

Isn't that carrying literary criticism a bit far?
AYATOLLAH SAYS: "KILL RUSHDIE"

I must do better,
I must do better,
I must do better,
I must do...

If it would help your cause, Sir - I'd be happy to go on strike..

One more day
and we could
have started
WORLD WAR 3...

I don't need technology to tell me you're dead drunk...
Are you using the LEFT or the RIGHT side of your brain?
Z Z Z

There's always

the LISTENING

DAD...

BANKS
WON'T
LEND
TO
STUDENTS

If I don't like this illness - can I PAY for a different one?

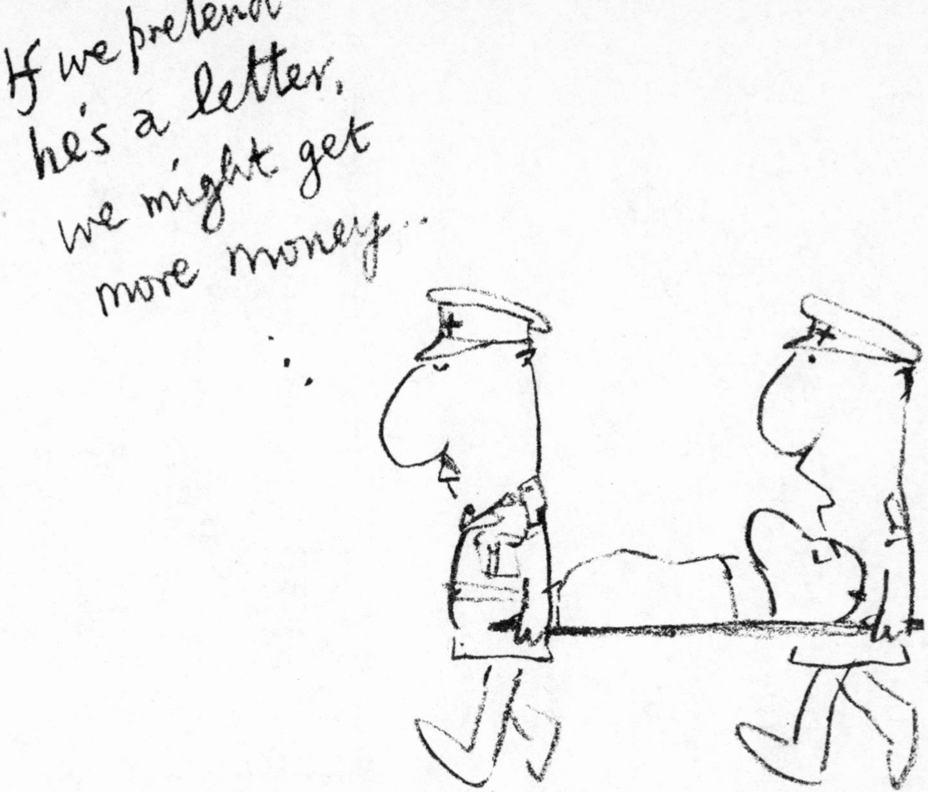
If we pretend he's a letter, we might get more money...

Can I have
the illness
you advertised
on TV?

Is the BABY
COMING OUT
in sympathy?

MIDWIVES
RESIGN!

Even maggie hasn't thought of that yet...
CEAUSESCU FIXED WEATHER

I can cope with going everywhere via PARIS...
B.R. MAY LOSE OUT TO FRENCH.

NOW CLOSED ON SUNDAYS
I shall now have to spend twice as much on Saturdays...

If everything's shut - we could go to CHURCH...
SUNDAY TRADING

First the BIRTH,
now worrying about the NAME –
I'm getting less SLEEP than
the FATHER...

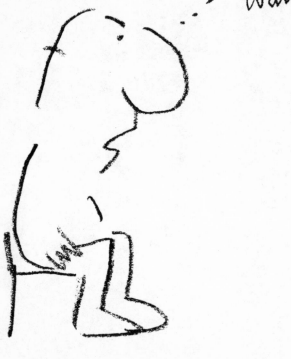

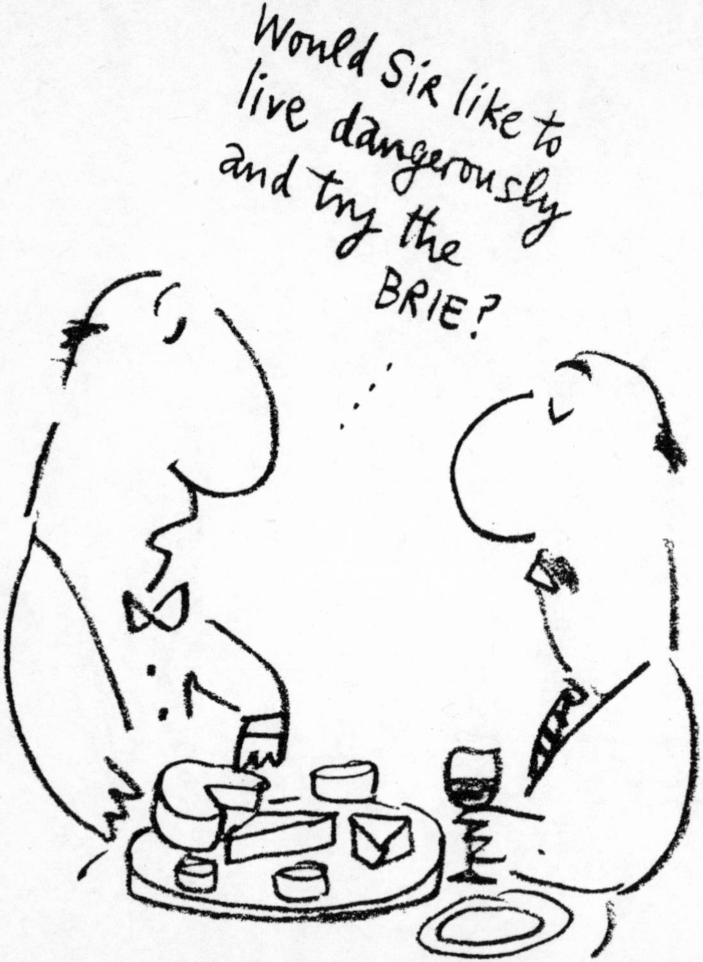
Would Sir like to live dangerously and try the BRIE?

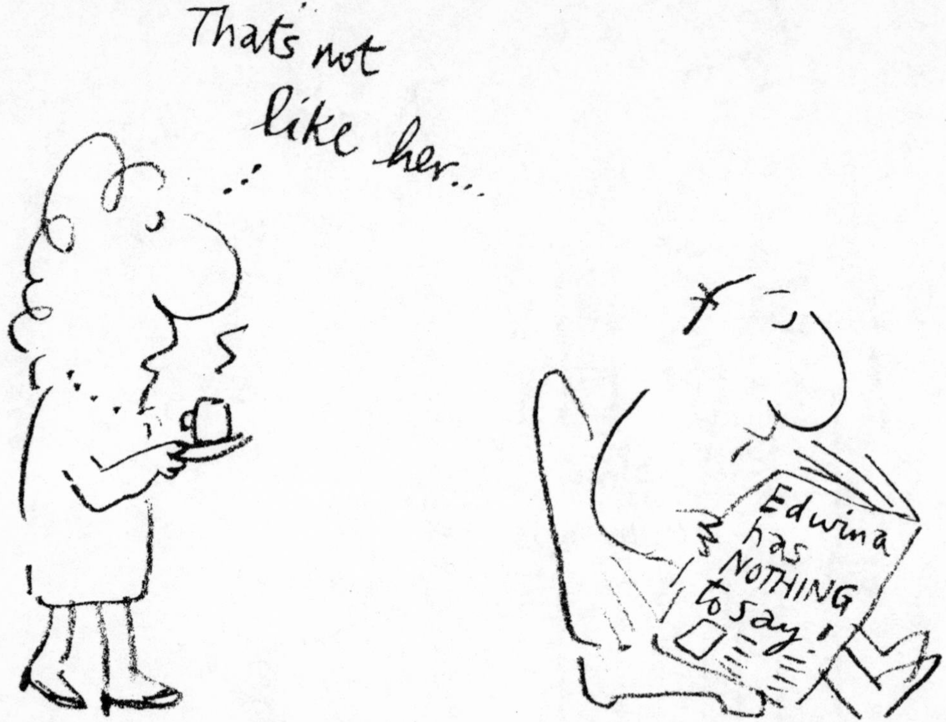
That's not like her...
Edwina has NOTHING to say!

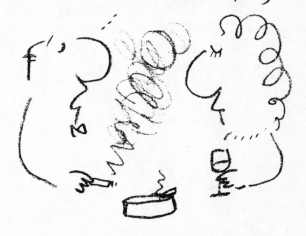

How are the old BOWEL MOVEMENTS today?
Terrific - I've just found this wonderful lift in our FLATS and it's BLISS - there's nothing to beat FITTED CARPET for helping the OLD COLON...

I used to go out but the streets are NOW so full of RUBBISH and LITTER - I can't FACE it!
I KNOW - HUMANS are SO DISGUSTING - I feel quite CONSTIPATED looking at them..

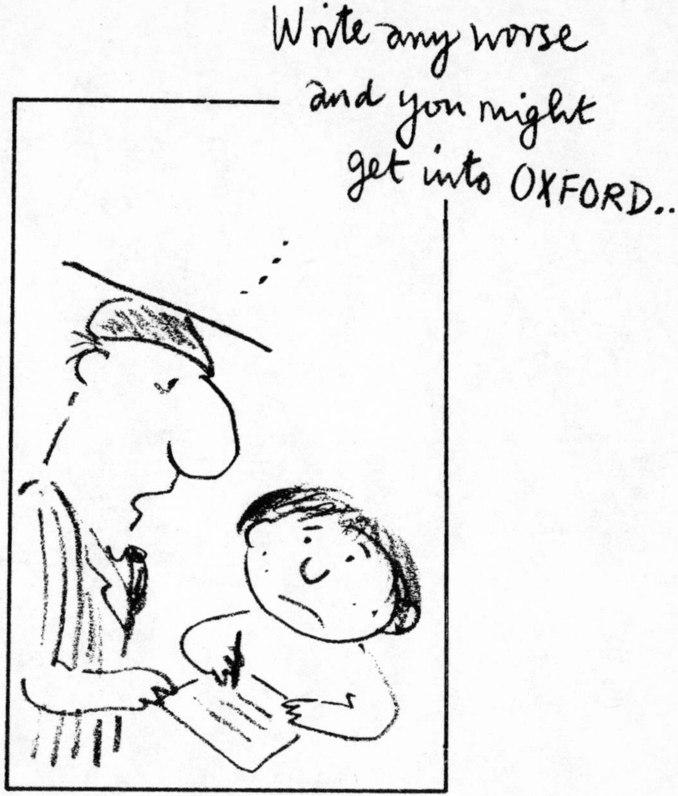
Write any worse
and you might
get into OXFORD...

You can't be much of a fan – you're SOBER!

He's the sort who gives soccer hooligans a bad name...
CLOUGH FINED.

TORY M.P's are
'REBELS' -
I'm just 'FED-UP'

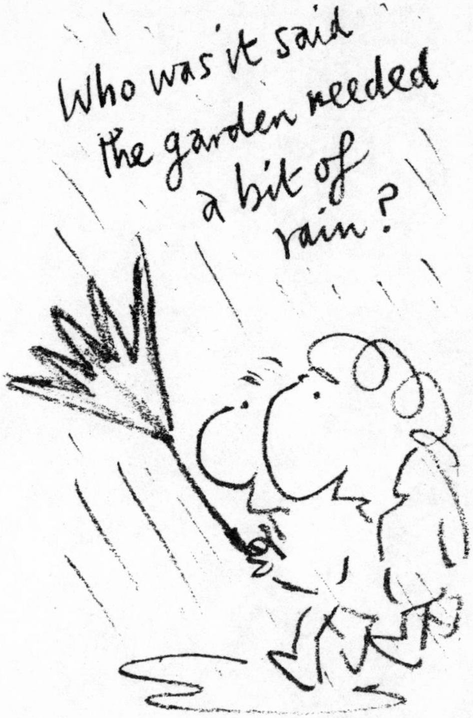
Who was it said
the garden needed
a bit of
rain?

Only people who UNDERSTAND it will have to PAY it ...
POLL TAX ETC
I wish I'd read it now ...
POLL TAX LEAFLET STOPPED.

I never thought I'd look back with pleasure to REAGAN'S speeches...
BUSH's SPEECH..
LIVE(?)
FROM

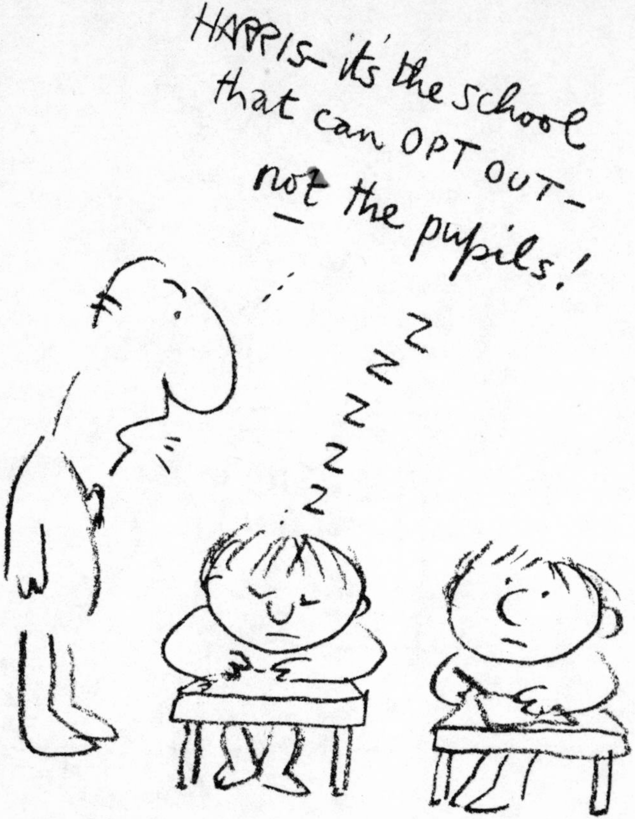
HARRIS– it's the school that can OPT OUT– not the pupils!
Z Z Z Z Z Z

What do you think of the WHITE PAPER on SECRETS?
I'm NOT allowed to say...
MP.
M.P.

I can't decide if
the clicking is
the POLICE, MI5,
or dear old
British
Telecom...

Psst – want a CUT-PRICE trial?
Tried any good TV programmes lately?

I'd like to put
an ELECTRONIC TAG
on you next time
you go to the PUB...

If I vote for you - will you MARRY me?
If you got EQUAL PAY - you could support me...

I think you can BUY a new toothbrush today without OVERHEATING the ECONOMY...
BOOM! BOOM! BOOM!

At least there'll be plenty to watch if we can't AFFORD to go out...
TV in the 1990's

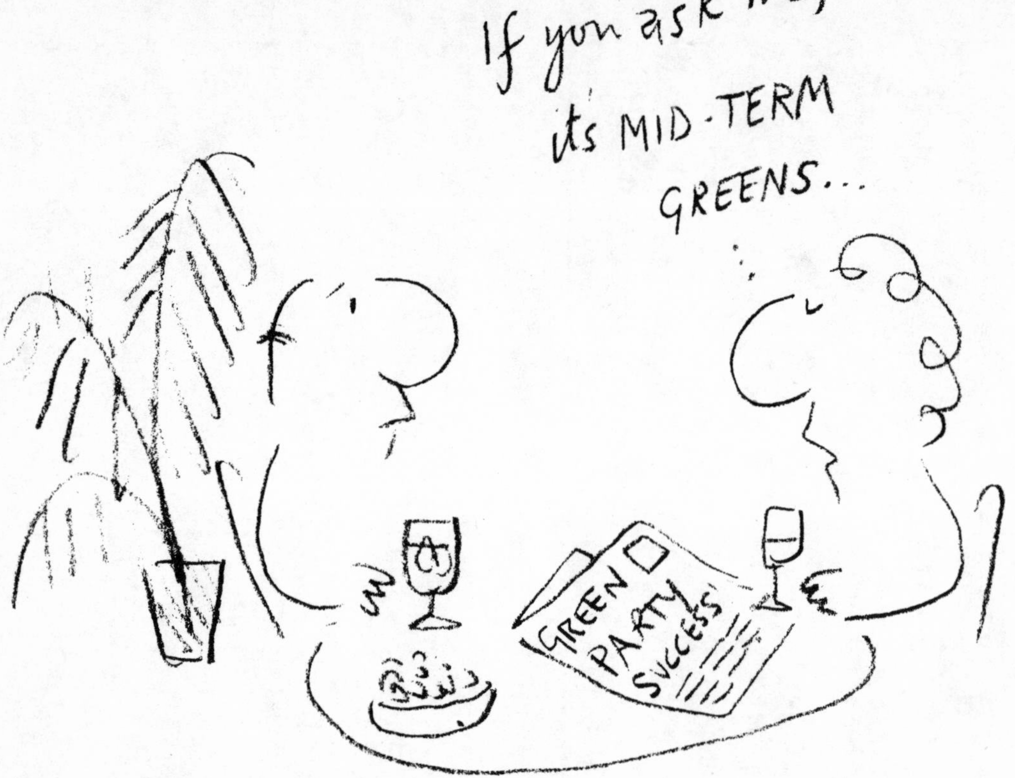
If you ask me,
its MID-TERM
GREENS...
GREEN PARTY SUCCESS

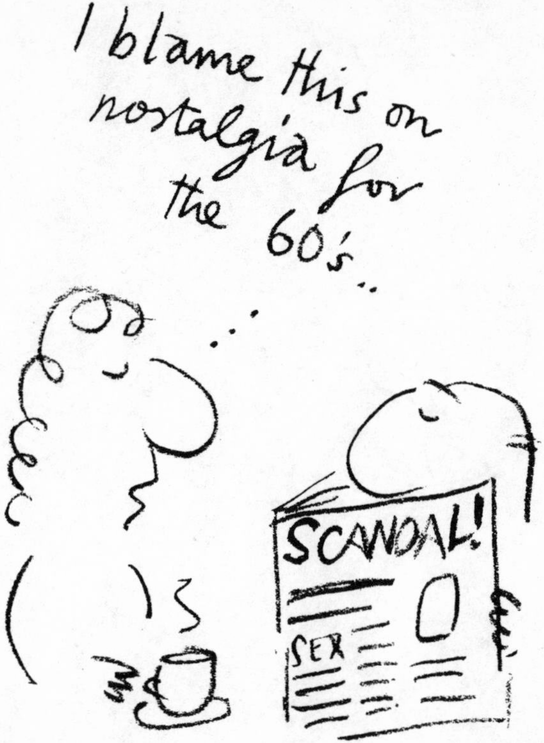
I blame this on nostalgia for the 60's...
SCANDAL!
SEX

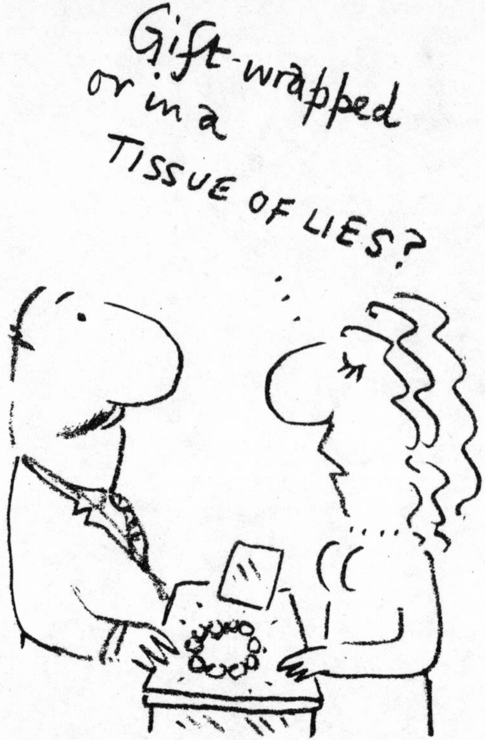
Gift-wrapped or in a TISSUE OF LIES?

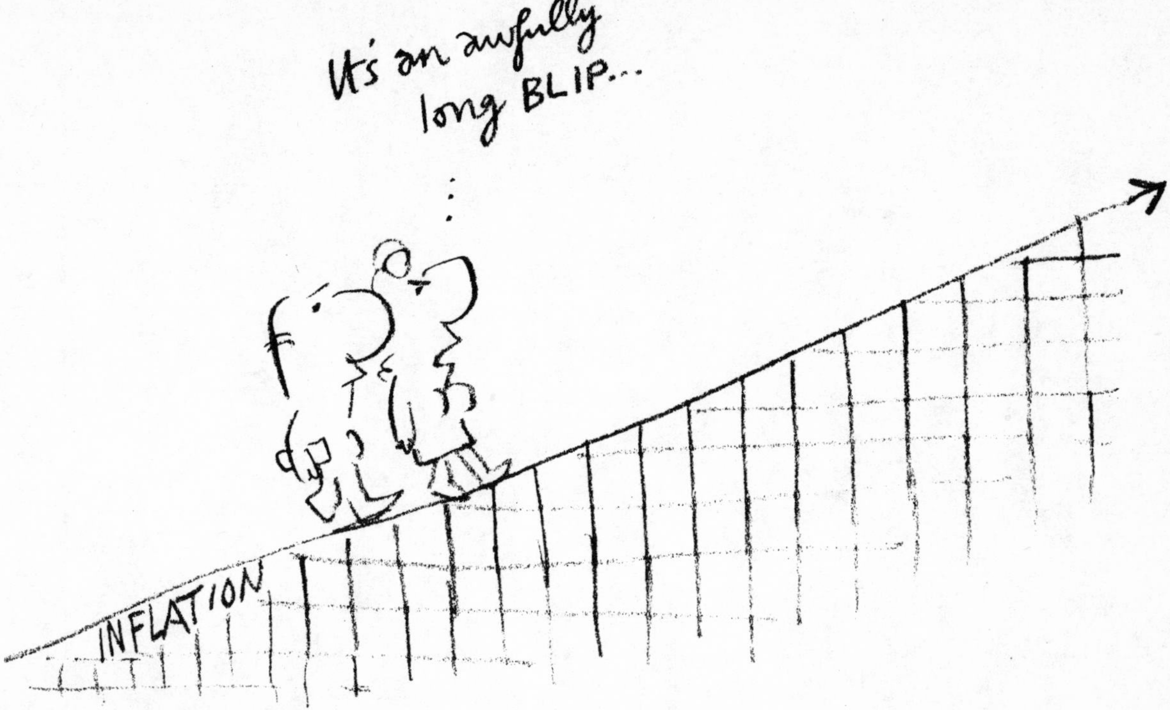
It's an awfully long BLIP...
INFLATION

The Government says
We're BETTER OFF —
pass it on...

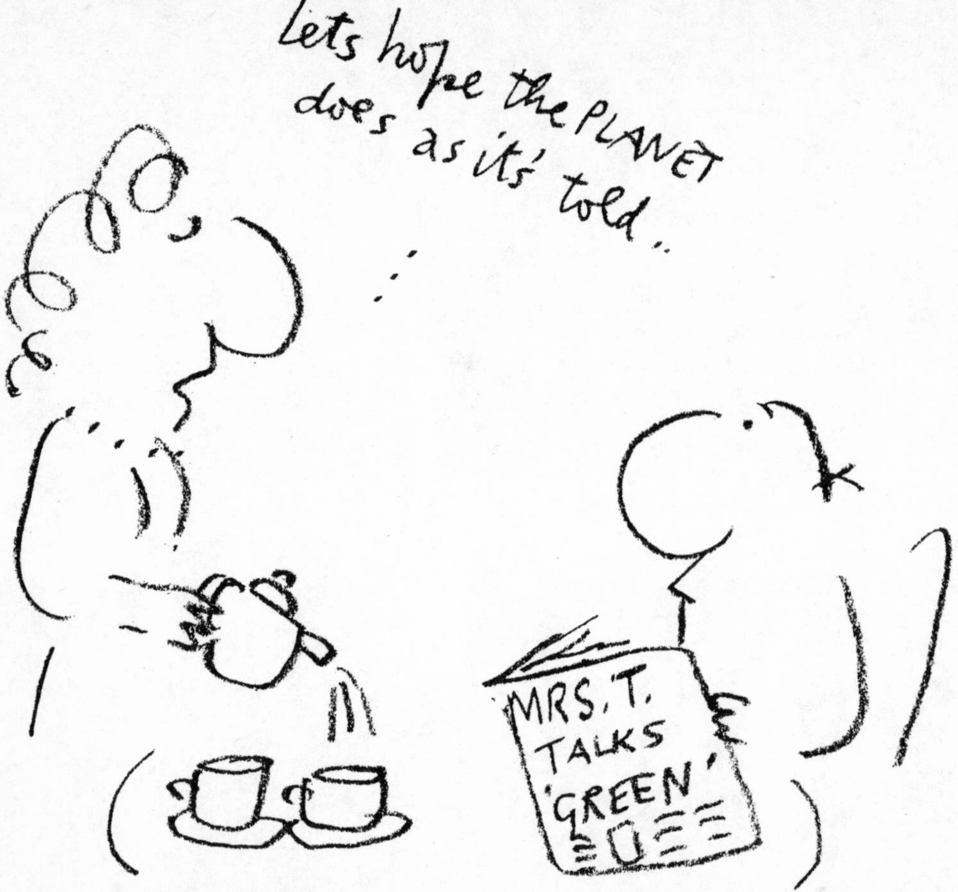
lets hope the PLANET does as it's told..
MRS. T. TALKS 'GREEN'

Anyone seen my FILOFAX?
I think you filed it under 'CLUTTER'..
I'm writing a piece for "TIME OUT" on AL FRESCO LIVING and I wondered if...
CAMDEN CARES
RING! RING!
FAST FOODS INC
LITTER HERE!
KEEP LONDON CLEAN
COKE
COKE

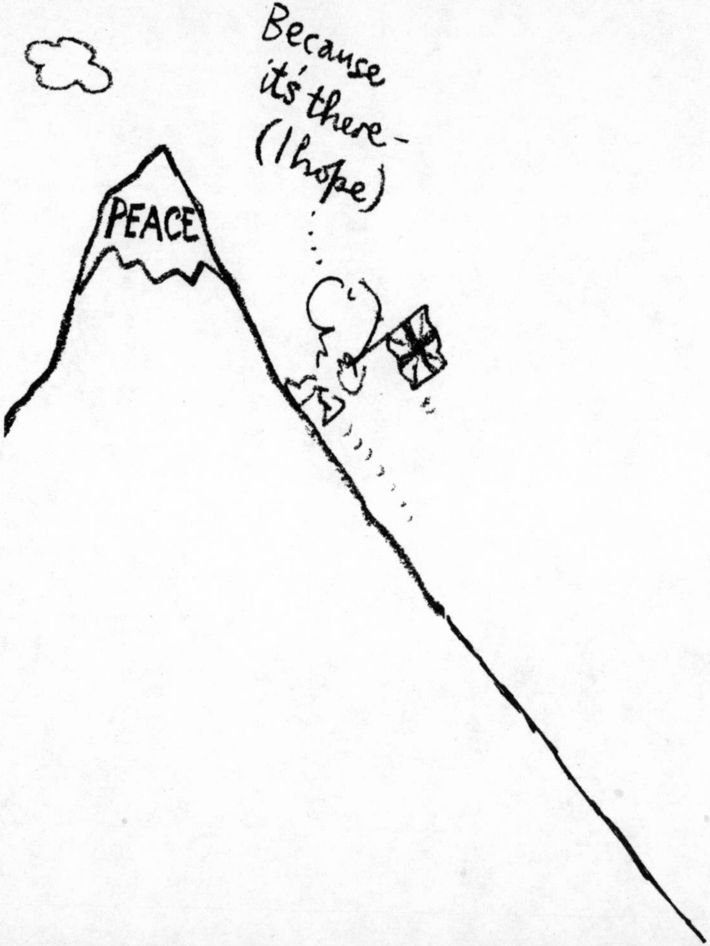
Because it's there - (I hope)
PEACE